# AMAZING MYSTERIES
# GHOULS

BY MELISSA GISH

T0015975

CREATIVE EDUCATION
CREATIVE PAPERBACKS

Published by Creative Education and Creative Paperbacks
P.O. Box 227, Mankato, Minnesota 56002
Creative Education and Creative Paperbacks are imprints of
The Creative Company
www.thecreativecompany.us

Design by The Design Lab
Production by Rachel Klimpel
Art direction by Rita Marshall
Printed in the United States of America

Photographs by Alamy (Elena Gladkaya, Kirsty Pargeter, mark
Turner), Creative Commons Wikimedia (Akseli Gallen-Kallela/Turku
Art Museum, Kawanabe Kyōsai, Sultan Muhammad/Ferdowsi/
Metropolitan Museum of Art, James Tissot), Getty Images (Dorling
Kindersley), Metropolitan Museum of Art (Mu'in Musavvir/Bequest
of Monroe C. Gutman, 1974), Shutterstock (danm12, e71lena,
Mikesilent, SugaBorn86, sutlafk, Warpaint), Unsplash.com (Jenny
Marvin)

Library of Congress Cataloging-in-Publication Data
Names: Gish, Melissa, author.
Title: Ghouls / Melissa Gish.
Series: Amazing mysteries.
Includes bibliographical references and index.
Summary: A basic exploration of the appearance, behaviors, and
origins of ghouls, the evil mythological creatures known for their
ability to cause pain. Also included is a story from folklore about a
ghoul tricking a traveler with a false light.

Identifiers:
ISBN 978-1-64026-489-2 (hardcover)
ISBN 978-1-68277-040-5 (pbk)
ISBN 978-1-64000-616-4 (eBook)
This title has been submitted for CIP processing under LCCN
2021937594.

First Edition HC 9 8 7 6 5 4 3 2 1
First Edition PBK 9 8 7 6 5 4 3 2 1

# Table of Contents

*The earliest stories about ghouls classed them with spirits called jinn.*

# Ghouls are evil creatures that cause people pain. People in **Mesopotamia** first told stories about them 4,000 years ago. Demons called *gallu* dragged people to the land of the dead.

**Mesopotamia** the area between the Tigris and Euphrates rivers where the earliest civilizations formed

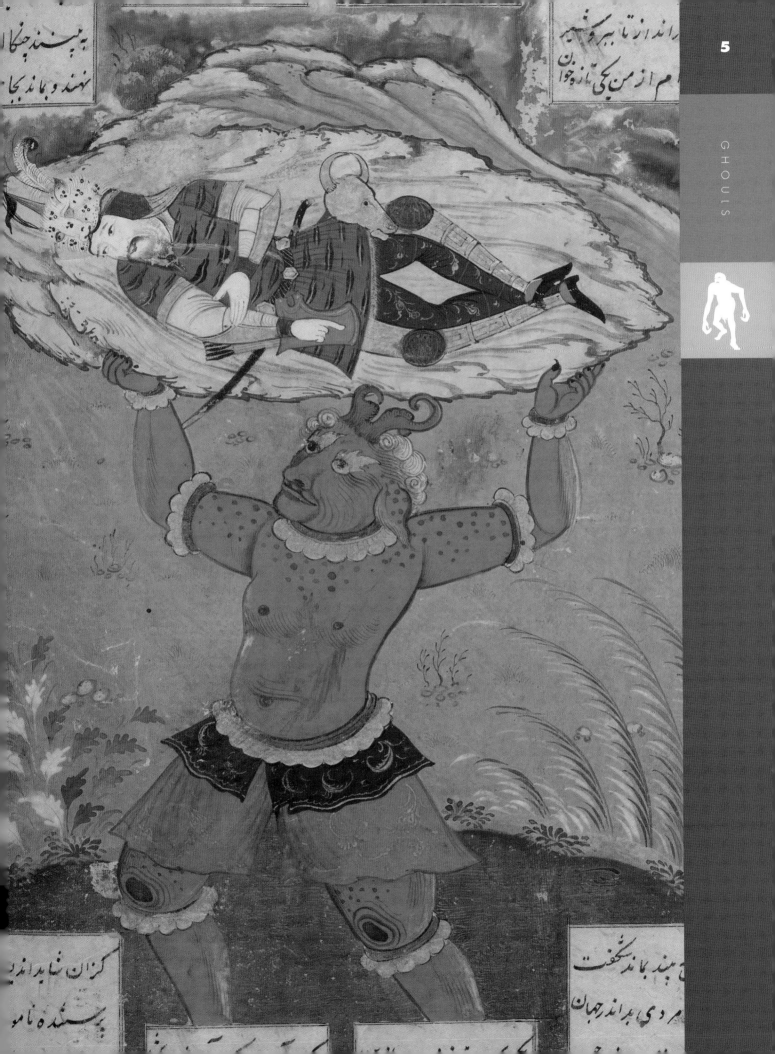

*Si'lwah and other witchlike creatures are common in many peoples' tales.*

In stories from ancient **Arabia**, ghouls are shape-changers. One early ghoul is the si'lwah (*si-LA*). It changes into a beautiful woman. She leads travelers away from their path. Then she attacks.

**Arabia** an area of land in southwestern Asia between the Red Sea and the Persian Gulf

A si'lwah may seem like a kindly traveler. It offers to carry tired children. Then it runs away with them! Parents must fight to get their children back. A sword strike can destroy a si'lwah.

*Striking a ghoul once was the only sure way to end its life.*

In the 1700s, the older Arabian stories were rewritten. *One Thousand and One Nights* told of ghouls creeping around graveyards and caves. Men trapped in a cave get out by blinding the ghoul.

*Places that seem creepy in the dark are often linked to scary monsters.*

# Some ghouls are hairy and move like animals. Others are humanlike. Their skin is pale. They have powerful claws. Big eyes help them to see in the dark. They groan and stink of rotten meat.

*Other demons, like Japan's oni (above), also have sharp claws.*

# Ghouls hide in dark places during the day. They dig up graves at night. They feast on the dead. They gnaw on bones with their sharp teeth. They lap up blood.

*The English word*
*ghoul comes from an*
*Arabic word meaning*
*"to seize."*

Some ghouls walk around, hunting the living. People who are bitten by ghouls become ghouls themselves.

*Ghouls have some things in common with other undead beings like vampires and zombies.*

No one knows for sure where ghouls come from. They may be helpers of demons. They may be the spirits of bad humans who have died. Or ghouls may have been created by the dark magic of witches.

*This painting from the 1500s shows someone defeating a group of demons.*

GHOULS

Some modern ghouls are harmless. In the book *The Lion, the Witch and the Wardrobe*, ghouls are the White Witch's trusty warriors. In the Harry Potter series, ghouls live in the attics and barns of wizards. They eat spiders and moths.

*Ideas about what makes a monster scary change over time.*

*A Ghoul Story*

# One night, a man went to visit his grandfather. A full moon lit his forest path. Clouds rolled in. Darkness fell. The man saw a light in the distance. Was it his grandfather's house? He turned his horse and traveled a long time. Then the light disappeared. The man was lost. A ghoul had tricked him with false light. The man could hear shuffling and groaning. The ghoul was coming for him!

# Read More

Ganeri, Anita. *Demons and Ghouls*. New York: PowerKids, 2011.

Lawrence, Sandra. *The Atlas of Monsters*. Philadelphia: Running Press Kids, 2019.

Tieck, Sarah. *Zombies*. Minneapolis: ABDO, 2016.

# Websites

How Stuff Works: Ghoul Biology 101
https://science.howstuffworks.com/science-vs-myth/strange-creatures
/ghoul1.htm
Read about the appearance and abilities of ghouls.

KidzSearch: Ghoul
https://wiki.kidzsearch.com/wiki/Ghoul
Learn about ghouls in literature and movies.

# Index